DOGBERT'S

CLUES FOR THE CLUELESS

Scott Adams

> DO WE HAVE ANY CLUELESS PEOPLE HERE TODAY ?

NICHOLAS BREALEY
PUBLISHING
L O N D O N

'To Sarah and Freddie and Freddie's Mom'

First published in Great Britain
by Nicholas Brealey Publishing Limited in 1993
36 John Street
London WC1N 2AT

Reprinted 1995, 1997 (three times)

© 1993 United Feature Syndicate, Inc.
Dogbert™ and Dilbert® appear daily in the DILBERT comic strip.

ISBN 1 85788 031 5

British Library Cataloguing in Publication Data
A catalogue record for this book is available from the British Library.

Printed and bound in Finland by Werner Söderström Oy

CONTENTS

Many years ago, a group of mischievous cave people were sitting in their little cave dwelling, chewing on dinosaur parts and thinking up cruel tricks to play on future generations. They decided it would be a major hoot to invent a whole bunch of inconvenient behaviors, teach them to their children and act as if it all made perfect sense.

Their plan was that when the children became adults — at about age six in those days — the elders would reveal their little joke, then roll around in their rancid fur loincloths, laughing until they got brain damage. Remember, this was before alcohol or cigarettes were invented. They were just being resourceful.

Anyway, before the adults could own up to their cruel hoax, they were all crushed by a stampede of frightened woolly mammoths who had accidentally walked across a carpet, thus generating the biggest wad of static electricity ever seen at that time. (You see, they were very woolly.)

So the children grew up never knowing that the moronic behaviors they learned from their parents were meant as a big joke. These behaviors were passed down from generation to generation, eventually being labeled "etiquette" because it sounds French, which makes sense for reasons I won't go into.

But lots of things have changed in the millions of years since etiquette was invented. Microwave ovens, for example. And so it seemed like a good time to update the rules of etiquette. That's why I wrote this book.

Of course, you could buy some other book on etiquette, and in it you might find such useful tidbits as what kind of uniform the upstairs servants should wear, or the proper way to address the Pope when you meet him in person. But if you want practical information — like what to do after you sneeze in your hand — then you have to buy this book. It's the only book that speaks to you as the unwashed heathen that you know you are.

Thanks. And I'm not just saying that.

Dogbert

EATING AND DRINKING

TALKING WITH YOUR MOUTH FULL

IN THE OLD DAYS, WHEN PEOPLE HAD MORE TIME, IT WAS IMPOLITE TO TALK WITH FOOD IN YOUR MOUTH.

NOW IT IS A NECESSITY.

THE FOAMING-AT-THE-MOUTH METHOD

WE DON'T SELL PRODUCTS; WE SELL <u>SOLUTIONS</u>.

J. Adams

THE SQUIRREL METHOD

SO THEN I SAID "THIS ISN'T MARKET-DRIVEN."

THIS METHOD IS STILL CONSIDERED IMPOLITE.

HEY! LOOK AT THOSE ENZYMES WORK! IS THIS INCREDIBLE OR WHAT?

TASTING WINE

HOW SHOULD YOU INDICATE TO THE WAITER THAT YOU DISAPPROVE OF THE WINE? THERE ARE THREE METHODS.

S. Adams

THE DOGBERT METHOD.

WE DON'T DRINK.

SPLAT

THE OVER-ACTING METHOD.

PHTOOO!!

DIVORCE

PRETEND YOU KNOW MORE THAN YOU DO.

I SUSPECT THE GRAPES WERE PICKED A DAY LATE.

THAT'S YOUR WATER GLASS, SIR.

THERE IS NO GOOD REASON TO WAIT FOR OTHER PEOPLE TO BE SERVED BEFORE YOU START EATING.

UNDER TRADITIONAL RULES OF ETIQUETTE EVERYBODY SITS AWKWARDLY UNTIL THE LAST PERSON IS SERVED.

YOUR SOUP WILL BE READY IN FEBRUARY.

THE DOGBERT METHOD TOTALLY ELIMINATES THE AWKWARD AND UNNECESSARY WAITING PERIOD.

DINNER CONVERSATION

CONFINE YOUR DINNER CONVERSATION TO THE ALLOWED TOPICS.

DON'T MENTION CERTAIN TOPICS WHEN EATING PASTA WITH TOMATO SAUCE.

I GAVE BLOOD TODAY. THEY COULDN'T FIND A VEIN.

DINNER TIME NEWS SHOWS ARE ALLOWED TO DISCUSS ANY THING, BECAUSE YOU "NEED TO KNOW."

...OUR SPECIAL REPORT ON ACCIDENTAL DISEMBOWELMENT.

HOWEVER ENJOYABLE, IT IS NEVER POLITE TO BE A WISE-ASS VEGETARIAN AT A COOKOUT.

AND HOW ABOUT THE COW'S BUTT — DO YOU THINK THEY JUST THROW THAT PART AWAY?

EATING OFF SOMEBODY ELSE'S PLATE

SOME RUDE PEOPLE WILL TRY TO EAT FROM YOUR PLATE. YOU HAVE THE RIGHT TO PROTECT WHAT IS YOURS.

WOW! FRENCH FRIES! I NEVER WOULD HAVE THOUGHT OF ORDERING SOMETHING I WANTED TO EAT!

S. Adams

YOUR FINER RESTAURANTS PROVIDE AN EXTRA FORK FOR DEFENDING YOUR PLATE.

EXAGGERATE YOUR HEALTH PROBLEMS.

THE DOCTOR CALLED IT BUBONIC SOME-THING-OR-OTHER. HE KEELED OVER BEFORE I COULD ASK ANY QUESTIONS.

RESTAURANTS AND SCREAMING KIDS

CHILDREN ARE EXEMPT FROM ETIQUETTE IN RESTAURANTS AND SO ARE THEIR PARENTS.

IT IS ACCEPTED PRACTICE TO BRING YOUR SCREAMING CHILD INTO FINE RESTAURANTS AND IGNORE HIM.

AAAAAAH!

IT IS NOT ACCEPTABLE TO USE YOUR TABLE BREAD TO MUFFLE THE NOISE.

WAITER, WE NEED MORE BREAD.

YOUR BEST BET IS TO BE DIRECT BUT BE GRACIOUS.

CHAMPAGNE AND A VASECTOMY, COMPLIMENTS OF TABLE THREE.

THE LAST PIECE OF BREAD

DRINKING FROM THE CONTAINER

REMEMBER THESE HELPFUL TIPS WHEN DRINKING ANYTHING FROM YOUR REFRIGERATOR.

WHEN PEOPLE ARE WATCHING, MAKE A BIG DEAL ABOUT USING A GLASS.

IT'S CALLED A "GLASS." I USE IT ALL THE TIME.

IF NOBODY IS LOOKING, YOU HAVE THE RIGHT TO DRINK THE ENTIRE CONTAINER WITHOUT USING YOUR HANDS.

HOWEVER, IT IS NEVER GOOD ETIQUETTE TO GIVE YOURSELF A SPONGE-BATH WITH ANY ITEM FROM THE REFRIGERATOR.

REFRESHING.

S. Adams

TIPPING THE WAITER

HERE ARE SOME TIPS ON TIPPING THAT YOU WON'T GET ANYWHERE ELSE.

IF THE SERVICE IS PROMPT BUT THE WAITER IS OBNOXIOUS, TOSS THE TIP ON THE FLOOR AND MAKE HIM CRAWL.

PENALIZE THE WAITER FOR POOR FOOD QUALITY OR ANYTHING ELSE THAT'S BOTHERING YOU LATELY.

MINUS A DOLLAR BECAUSE PEOPLE TAILGATE.

TIP IN ADVANCE IF YOU HAVE ANY SPECIAL REQUESTS.

HERE'S A BUCK. STOP MAKING CLEVER CONVERSATION WITH US.

S.Adams

VEGETARIAN ETIQUETTE

IF YOU HAVE WEIRD VEGETARIAN FRIENDS IT IS BEST NOT TO INVITE THEM TO A BARBECUE.

JIMBO! GLAD YOU COULD MAKE IT! HELP YOURSELF TO THE DOLPHIN SALAD!

THIS MAY SEEM PRIMITIVE TO YOU, JIM, BUT I BELIEVE THE LOWER FORMS OF LIFE ARE MEANT TO BE EATEN.

POOR TONY ONLY SCORED A COMBINED 700 ON HIS S.A.T...

WATER FOUNTAINS

IT IS RUDE TO TOUCH A PUBLIC WATER FOUNTAIN WITH YOUR LIPS, UNLESS YOU HAVE DEVELOPED A RELATIONSHIP WITH IT.

S. Adams

RUDE

SLURP GURGLE

VERY RUDE!

SLURP GURGLE

CORRECT

ALTHOUGH I HAVEN'T KNOWN YOU LONG, ALREADY I'M THIRSTY.

WHEN WOMEN PAY FOR DINNER

MANY MEN ARE STILL UNCOMFORTABLE WHEN A WOMAN INSISTS ON PICKING UP THE CHECK. FOR THE MAN, THERE IS ONLY ONE CORRECT RESPONSE.

WRONG*: HITTING HER WITH THE BUTT OF YOUR GUN.

* EXCEPT IN UTAH

WRONG: TRYING HUMOR TO LIGHTEN THE TENSION.

NOW I GUESS I'LL HAVE TO SLEEP WITH YOU! HAW HAW!

CORRECT: RETURN TO THE OCEAN LIKE THE JELLYFISH YOU'VE BECOME.

S.Adams

MANNERS FOR SINGLE EATERS

JUST BECAUSE YOU EAT ALONE IS NO REASON TO ABANDON GOOD MANNERS.

WHEN EATING A DONUT OVER THE KITCHEN SINK, HUNCH THE BACK AND KEEP AN ELBOW OUT.

ELBOW OUT

IT IS OKAY TO EAT A POTATO CHIP THAT FALLS ON YOUR CHEST BUT NOT ONE THAT FALLS IN THE COUCH CRACK.

OKAY

NO

CHIP

NAPKINS ARE UNNECESSARY IF YOU PLAN TO TAKE A SHOWER IN THE MORNING ANYWAY.

S. Adams

EMPLOYEE EGOS

IT IS BAD FORM TO DISCUSS YOUR SUPERIOR LIFE IN FRONT OF LOWER LEVEL EMPLOYEES.

S. Adams

DON'T TALK ABOUT YOUR INCOME.

ALL I DID WAS WALK AROUND TODAY... AND I MADE TWICE YOUR SALARY.

DON'T TALK ABOUT THEIR CUBICLES.

THIS CUBICLE REMINDS ME OF THE CARDBOARD BOX THAT MY BIG SCREEN TV CAME IN.

DON'T TALK ABOUT YOUR ACCESS TO A MORE BOUNTIFUL SEX LIFE.

I THINK I'LL GO USE MY POSITION OF POWER AS AN APHRODISIAC.

BEING LATE FOR MEETINGS

THE ACCEPTABLE LEVEL OF LATENESS FOR A MEETING DEPENDS ON WHAT YOU THINK OF THE OTHER ATTENDEES.

YOU CAN BE SEVEN MINUTES LATE FOR A MEETING WITH CO-WORKERS FOR WHOM YOU HAVE NO REAL RESPECT.

I WAS DOING MY MAIL.

YOU CAN BE FIFTEEN MINUTES LATE FOR A MEETING WITH PEOPLE WHO ARE — IN YOUR OPINION — FETID PILES OF GARBAGE.

I FORGOT TO LOOK AT MY CALENDAR.

IF YOU'RE AN IMPORTANT EXECUTIVE YOU CAN BE AN HOUR LATE, BECAUSE TO YOU ALL THE EMPLOYEES LOOK LIKE FETID GARBAGE WITH BAD ATTITUDES.

I'D TELL YOU WHY I'M LATE BUT YOU WOULDN'T UNDERSTAND

S. Adams

ELEVATOR EFFICIENCY

POLITE BEHAVIOR IN ELEVATORS CAN SERIOUSLY IMPACT YOUR SCHEDULE. USE THESE TRICKS TO BE MORE EFFICIENT.

SCOWL AT THOSE WHO TAKE THE ELEVATOR FOR ONE FLOOR; IT MAY REDUCE FUTURE ABUSES.

STAND DIRECTLY IN FRONT OF THE ELEVATOR AS THOUGH YOU ARE THE ONLY PERSON ON EARTH.

YOU DON'T HAVE TO HOLD THE ELEVATOR IF YOU PRETEND YOU DON'T SEE ANYBODY COMING.

ELEVATOR ETIQUETTE

THERE ARE SOME THINGS YOU SHOULD NEVER DO ON AN ELEVATOR.

NEVER FACE THE BACK. IT MAKES PEOPLE NERVOUS.

NEVER STAND NEXT TO A PERSON IF THERE ARE ONLY TWO OF YOU.

DON'T TRY TO CRUSH PEOPLE BY PUSHING THE "CLOSE" BUTTON. I'VE TRIED IT AND IT DOESN'T WORK.

CLOSE

MY SECRETARY THE BOSS

YOU MAY DEBASE YOUR SECRETARY BY WHIMSIC- ALLY REFERRING TO HIM OR HER AS YOUR "BOSS."

BEFORE WE START, LET'S GO AROUND THE TABLE AND INTRODUCE OURSELVES.

S. Adams

I'M LARRY, AND I WORK FOR IRENE ... HEH, HEH...

REALLY?

HA HA

HOWEVER, THERE IS A DANGER THAT THIS WILL CONFUSE PEOPLE.

YES! MY HARD WORK PAID OFF AND I DIDN'T EVEN KNOW IT. GET ME SOME COFFEE, YOU POMPOUS REAR-END!

THE LAST DONUT

IT IS IMPOLITE TO TAKE THE LAST DONUT WITHOUT OFFERING IT TO OTHERS FIRST. USE THESE TRICKS TO MAKE SURE THEY DON'T TAKE IT.

YOU TAKE IT, BETH. IT'LL HELP YOU KEEP THAT RUBENESQUE FIGURE.

HOW ABOUT YOU, WALLY? WE ALL LOVE TO WATCH THE WAY YOU EAT!

LATECOMERS TO THE MEETING ARE HARDER TO CONTROL.

DIG IN, I THINK THE FLIES GOT ALL THEY WANTED ON THIS ONE.

MANNERS AND YOUR BODY

SNEEZING IN YOUR HAND

IF SOMEBODY WANTS TO SHAKE HANDS SOON AFTER YOU SNEEZED IN YOUR HAND, YOU HAVE THREE OPTIONS.

AAAACHOO !!!

THOUGHTFUL

OOH, BETTER NOT. I SNEEZED IN MY HAND.

PLAYFUL

BAD TIMING, BOB.

DOGBERTFUL

PARDON MY DAMP PAW; I JUST WASHED IT.

HE'S BOTH CLEAN AND POLITE.

S.Adams

SPITTERS

THERE ARE NO GRACEFUL METHODS FOR DEALING WITH PEOPLE WHO SPIT WHEN THEY TALK.

IMAGINE YOURSELF STANDING ON THE BEACH AND FEELING THE COOL OCEAN SPRAY.

BLAH BLAH BLAH

BUILD A "CONE OF DRYNESS"

BLAH BLAH BLAH

SPIT BACK, BUT MAKE IT LOOK LIKE AN ACCIDENT

BLAH BLAH BLAH

BLAH BLAH BLAH!!

BREAST FEEDING

WHEN WOMEN BREAST-FEED BABIES IN PUBLIC YOU MUST TRY TO ACT LIKE IT DOESN'T BOTHER YOU.

MAKE WITTY COMMENTS.

HEY, WHERE'S THE LINE FORM?

S. Adams

NONCHALANTLY EXCUSE YOUR-SELF FROM THE ROOM.

I THINK I'LL SEE WHAT'S ON THE BOOB TUBE.

TRY TO ONE-UP HER.

THOSE FLOWERS LOOK LIKE THEY NEED WATERING.

YAWNING

REMEMBER THESE HANDY TIPS ON YAWNING.

TRY THE ONE-NOSTRIL SECRET YAWN METHOD.

S. Adams

COVER YOUR MOUTH SO NOBODY CAN TELL THAT YOU YAWNED.

I WONDER IF HE'S YAWNING BEHIND THAT HAND.

AAAAHH!

FOR YOUR MORE VIGOROUS YAWNS, TRY NOT TO CATCH OTHER PEOPLE IN YOUR VORTEX.

OOPS

THE SOUNDS OF EATING

FOR REASONS UNKNOWN, IT IS IMPOLITE TO MAKE SOUNDS WHILE EATING, EXCEPT IN SOME CULTURES.

S. Adams

E-E-E-RP!! OH, EXCUSE ME.

IN MY COUNTRY A BURP IS CONSIDERED A COMPLIMENT.

FRRP

I SUPPOSE THAT WAS TOO MUCH TO HOPE FOR.

BAD BREATH

IF YOU KNOW SOMEBODY WHO HAS BAD BREATH, THERE ARE THREE WAYS TO TELL HIM.

THE CLEVER APPROACH

HEY, TODD, DID SOME KIND OF ANIMAL CRAWL IN YOUR MOUTH AND DIE?

LEAVE SUBTLE CLUES AND LET THE OFFENDER DEDUCE IT ON HIS OWN.

WHICH ITEM DOES NOT BELONG ON THIS LIST?

SKUNK   TODD'S MOUTH   DAISY

THE SCIENTIFIC METHOD

NOW, TODD, CAN YOU GUESS WHAT MADE THIS LITTLE EXPERIMENT WORK?

SITTING ON "THEM" (MEN ONLY)

SOMETIMES THE COMBINATION OF TEMPERATURE AND ILL-FITTING CLOTHES CAUSES A GUY TO SIT AND SCRUNCH "THEM" IN MIXED COMPANY. HE HAS THREE OPTIONS.

TOUGH IT OUT

DIVERT AND CORRECT

WHAT <u>IS</u> THAT UP THERE??

EXPLAIN, THEN CORRECT (NOT RECOMMENDED)

IN A MOMENT, I'M GOING TO DO SOMETHING THAT MAY SEEM UNUSUAL...

S. Adams

NUDITY

THIS IS A SENSITIVE TOPIC, SO I'LL DEAL WITH IT IN A DELICATE AND DIGNIFIED MANNER.

S. Adams

IT IS EQUALLY IMPOLITE FOR ANIMALS TO WEAR PANTS AS IT IS FOR PEOPLE TO BE NUDE.

SOME EXCEPTIONS INCLUDE HAIRLESS MANX CATS WHO MUST WEAR PANTS AND, IDEALLY, A PAPER BAG...

MEOW

MEN WITH HAIRY BACKS ARE REQUIRED BY GOOD ETIQUETTE TO MOVE TO TIBET AND LIVE AS YETIS.

NUDITY

THE CORRECT AMOUNT OF CLOTHING DEPENDS ON CUSTOM, CONTEXT, AND GOOD JUDGEMENT.

S. Adams

FOR EXAMPLE, A WELL-DRESSED MUMMY SHOULD COVER THE ENTIRE BODY.

BUT A BEACH-GOER CAN WEAR AS LITTLE AS A THONG BIKINI.

HOWEVER, A MUMMY SHOULD NEVER WEAR A BIKINI.

LOOKING GOOD...

RUDENESS WARNING SIGNS

RATHER THAN MEMORIZING THE MANY RULES OF ETIQUETTE YOU CAN USE THESE SIMPLE EARLY WARNING INDICATORS TO AVOID RUDENESS.

S. Adams

IF YOUR LIPS ARE EXTENDED BEYOND YOUR NOSE THEN YOU ARE ABOUT TO DO SOMETHING RUDE.

POSSIBLE SLURP IN PROGRESS.

IF A LOUD NOISE IS ABOUT TO COME OUT OF YOUR BODY — AND IT IS NOT LANGUAGE — THEN YOU ARE ABOUT TO BE RUDE.

POSSIBLE BURP, SNEEZE, OR WORSE.

IF YOU USE SOMETHING FOR OTHER THAN ITS INTENDED PURPOSE YOU MAY ALREADY BE RUDE.

HONK!!

PERSONAL SPACE

YOUR PERSONAL SPACE REQUIREMENTS DEPEND ON YOUR CULTURAL INFLUENCES.

S. Adams

IN ITALY YOU MAY GET INSIDE ANOTHER PERSON'S CLOTHES.

HI, I'M MARIO.

IN THE UNITED STATES YOU ARE ALLOWED JUST INSIDE THE BAD BREATH ZONE.

BAD BREATH ZONE

IN AUSTRALIA ANY DISTANCE IS TOO DANG CLOSE.

HEY! CAN WE TALK?!

HE MUST BE A TOURIST.

MEN AND WOMEN

GREETING CARD DISPOSAL

MEN AND WOMEN HAVE DIFFERENT ACCEPTED STANDARDS FOR HOW LONG TO KEEP A GREETING CARD.

FEMALE STANDARD

OH MY GOD, IT'S SO BEAUTIFUL! I SHALL KEEP IT ALWAYS.

$1.75

MALE STANDARD

HAPPY TENTH ANNIVERSARY, HONEY.

I LOVE YOU ♡

STUFF STUFF STUFF

S. Adams

DOUBLE DOOR DILEMMA

HOLDING DOORS CAN BE COMPLICATED IF YOU ENCOUNTER THEM IN PAIRS.

S. Adams

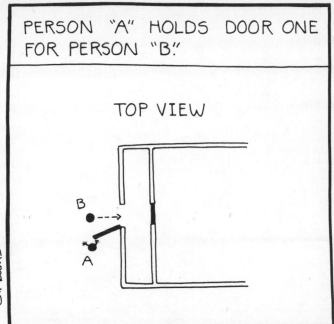

PERSON "A" HOLDS DOOR ONE FOR PERSON "B."

TOP VIEW

PERSON "B" SCURRIES TO DOOR TWO AND HOLDS IT FOR PERSON "A."

TOP VIEW

ACTUALLY, THIS ONLY APPLIES TO DORKY MALES, WHO ARE ALSO REQUIRED BY LAW TO MAKE STUPID FACES AND SAY...

AGE BEFORE BEAUTY!

KEEPING YOUR SEAT (FOR MEN)

OFTEN IT IS THE MAN WHO IS EXPECTED TO GIVE UP HIS SEAT ON PUBLIC TRANSPORTATION. USE THESE TRICKS TO KEEP YOURS.

PRETEND TO BE ASLEEP.

ACT CRAZY AND MAYBE SOMEBODY ELSE WILL MOVE.

USE PSYCHOLOGY TO INSTILL A GREATER SENSE OF GUILT IN SOMEBODY ELSE.

SO, WHAT DO YOU THINK OF THE WOMEN'S MOVEMENT?

LETTING HIM WIN

IN LESS ENLIGHTENED DAYS IT WAS POLITE FOR A WOMAN TO LET A MAN WIN AT SPORTS.

BUT THOSE DAYS ARE GONE

S. Adams

OLD METHOD

I THINK I HIT ONE OF THEM!

NEW METHOD

I LOVE THE SOUND THAT MAKES.

FUTURE METHOD

ALL I'M SAYING IS THAT WE COULD TAKE TURNS. WE DON'T ALWAYS HAVE TO KICK-BOX TO DECIDE WHO PAYS FOR THE MOVIE.

WOMEN'S LEG HAIR

WOMEN ARE SENSITIVE WHEN THEY HAVEN'T HAD TIME TO SHAVE THEIR LEGS. BE CAREFUL.

DO NOT TRY TO MAKE THE BEST OUT OF THE SITUATION.

WE'RE OUT OF SANDPAPER, AND I NEED TO TAKE THE EDGE OFF THIS BREAD BOARD, SO I WAS THINKING...

S. Adams

DON'T NAG.

WELL, GREAT, NOW YOU'VE KILLED THE CAT.

WHEN SHE WANTS TO SPOON, TAKE IT LIKE A MAN.

HELP!! HELP!!

COMPLIMENTING A WOMAN

THE PROPER METHOD FOR COMPLIMENTING A WOMAN ON HER APPEARANCE DEPENDS ON YOUR SOCIAL AND ECONOMIC STATUS.

S. Adams

THE WEALTHY

I SIMPLY MUST HAVE THE NAME OF YOUR PLASTIC SURGEON.

I'M FLATTERED.

MIDDLE CLASS

THAT OUTFIT LOOKS GOOD ON YOU.

LAWSUIT

LOWER CLASS

NICE HOOTERS.

THANKS.

FLIRTING

CASUAL FLIRTING IS ACCEPTABLE, BUT YOU SHOULD AVOID THESE EXTREMES.

IT IS RUDE TO ACTIVELY ENCOURAGE FLIRTERS WHILE ON A DATE.

GOOD, GOOD. NOW DO THIS ONE.

IT IS RUDE TO NEGOTIATE IN FRONT OF YOUR DATE.

IF YOU'RE INTERESTED, I COULD BREAK IT OFF WITH HIM RIGHT NOW.

AND IT IS VERY RUDE TO ACT LIKE YOUR DATE DOESN'T EVEN EXIST.

FIVE MORE MINUTES AND YOU CAN JUST FORGET THE MOVIE.

HUSBAND REVENGE

HUSBANDS MAY ANNOY WIVES WITHOUT BEING RUDE IF THEY FOLLOW THESE TIME-TESTED METHODS.

CLICK

CHANGE CHANNELS QUICKLY AND CONSTANTLY AS IF YOU WILL NEVER STOP.

CLICK CLICK CLICK CLICK CLICK CLICK CLICK CLICK CLICK CLICK CLICK

BUY TOOLS FOR THINGS SHE DIDN'T EVEN KNOW YOU NEEDED A TOOL FOR.

I NEEDED IT TO DEMAGNETIZE THE RAIN GUTTERS.

BECOME UNUSUALLY ANIMATED AND ATTENTIVE IN THE PRESENCE OF ATTRACTIVE WOMEN.

KISSING AND TELLING

IT'S OKAY TO KISS AND TELL, AS LONG AS YOU OBSERVE SOME SIMPLE RULES OF TACT.

WAIT AWHILE. DON'T TELL RIGHT AWAY.

I'M SERIOUS, MONICA. IT WAS LIKE KISSING A SQUID...

A DESCRIPTION IS SUFFICIENT. THERE'S NO NEED TO RE-ENACT THE EVENT.

THEN ONE OF US STARTED KISSING LIKE THIS.

DON'T TELL YOUR UNATTACHED MALE FRIENDS. IT'S CRUEL.

I'M GLAD I HAVE A FRIEND WHO LISTENS TO MY ROMANCE STORIES IN ALL THEIR BORING DETAIL.

KNEE ROOM

WHEN A BIG UGLY MAN STEALS A WOMAN'S KNEE SPACE, THE WOMAN HAS THREE ALTERNATIVES.

AVOIDANCE AND THOUGHTS OF VIOLENCE

EXPLAIN THE SITUATION CLEARLY AND APPEAL TO HIS SENSE OF SOCIAL EQUITY. (NOT RECOMMENDED)

SHE WANTS ME. MY PLAN IS WORKING.

IMAGINE AN INVISIBLE LINE BETWEEN OUR SEATS...

ACCIDENTAL SODA SPILL

OOPS! SORRY! SOMEBODY BUMPED MY KNEE.

MEN HUGGING MEN

IN WESTERN CULTURES, WHEN HETEROSEXUAL MEN HUG THEY MUST OBSERVE CERTAIN CONVENTIONS.

KEEP THE NAUGHTY PARTS AT LEAST FOUR FEET AWAY.

DO NOT USE THE OPPORTUNITY TO REVEAL YOUR FEMININE SIDE.

DON'T LET ANYBODY SEE YOU GET THE HEEBIE-JEEBIES AFTERWARD.

POLITE TURN-DOWN LIES

WOMEN SHOULD USE POLITE LIES TO REJECT UNACCEPTABLE SUITORS.

NEARLY-NORMAL GUYS DESERVE VAGUE YET PLAUSIBLE LIES.

I'M SORRY, I HAVE "PLANS" THIS WEEKEND.

LOSER-TYPE GUYS CAN BE DISMISSED WITH SPECIFIC YET IMPLAUSIBLE LIES.

I HAVE TO WAX MY CAT.

BUT FOR THE TRULY PATHETIC, IT IS ACCEPTABLE TO USE SADISTIC AND MALICIOUS LIES.

WAIT BY THE PHONE. I'LL CALL SOMETIME BEFORE SATURDAY TO LET YOU KNOW.

OH BOY! OH BOY!

S. Adams

PREGNANCY AND WEIGHT

PREGNANT WOMEN CAN BE SENSITIVE ABOUT WEIGHT GAIN. DO NOT MAKE THESE MISTAKES.

WHEN'S THE BABY DUE? TOMORROW?

IN SEVEN MONTHS.

AH, MUST BE TWINS, RIGHT?

NOPE.

WHEN YOU'RE "EATING FOR TWO" HAVE YOU CONSIDERED THAT THE BABY IS ABOUT THE SIZE OF A GOLF BALL?

PUBLIC DISPLAYS OF AFFECTION

DEPENDING ON HOW ATTRACTIVE YOU ARE, PEOPLE WILL EXPERIENCE VARYING LEVELS OF REVULSION AT YOUR "PDA."

BEAUTIFUL PEOPLE HAVE NO LIMITS.

AVERAGE LOOKING PEOPLE SHOULD AVOID TOUCHING LIPS IN PUBLIC.

THE REST OF YOU HAD BETTER NOT RISK IT AT ALL.

SAYING NO TO A DANCE

IF AN UNDESIRABLE PERSON ASKS YOU TO DANCE, USE THESE METHODS TO POLITELY EXTRACT YOURSELF.

PRETEND YOU DON'T KNOW THE LANGUAGE.

MAY I HAVE THIS DANCE?

QUACK QUACK QUACK QUACK QUACK

SPILL YOUR DRINK ON HIS PANTS.

THIRD TIME TONIGHT. IT CAN'T BE A COINCIDENCE.

SPLASH

FIND A SACRIFICIAL DANCER TO TAKE YOUR PLACE.

SHARING YOUR DREAMS

DO NOT TELL PEOPLE WHAT ROLE THEY PLAYED IN YOUR DREAMS, NO MATTER HOW MEANINGLESS IT SEEMED TO YOU.

S. Adams

DILBERT, I HAD A FASCINATING DREAM ABOUT YOU LAST NIGHT.

I DREAMED IT WAS A BEAUTIFUL SUMMER EVENING. THE MOON WAS FULL...

YOU APPEARED AS A FIELD RODENT. I CRUSHED YOU WITH A BIG FLAT ROCK.

THANKS FOR TELLING ME.

STARING

IT IS IMPOLITE FOR A MAN TO GET CAUGHT STARING AT A WOMAN. MEN MUST USE THESE TRICKS TO AVOID DETECTION.

S. Adams

EXORCIST METHOD

USE REFLECTIVE SURFACES

CLEVER DECOY METHOD

WHERE DID YOU GET THAT NICE NECKLACE?

THREE "MOODS" OF THE MONTH

TO MEN, IT MAY SEEM THAT WOMEN HAVE THREE DISTINCT MOODS PER MONTH. THIS IS ONLY A MALE MYTH AND SHOULD NEVER BE MENTIONED.

"PRE"

STUPID BASTARD

"DURING"

I DIDN'T MEAN TO MENTION BLIMPS!! WE CAN TALK ABOUT SOMETHING ELSE!!

INSENSITIVE BASTARD.

"DENIAL"

YOU SEEMED A BIT MOODY YESTERDAY.

NO I WASN'T.

BASTARD

WIFE REVENGE

THE FOLLOWING ACTS ARE STILL PERMISSIBLE BUT THEY'VE BEEN ADDED TO THE WATCH LIST.

PUT YOUR COLD FEET ON HIM.

COOK LARGE QUANTITIES OF SOMETHING HIDEOUS AND MAKE IT CLEAR THAT YOU FEEL "VULNERABLE" TONIGHT.

IT'S OKAY IF YOU DON'T LIKE IT.

ASK HIM TO PICK UP SOME PERSONAL ITEMS AT THE STORE.

AFTER GOLF, WOULD YOU MIND STOPPING AT THE STORE?

WOMEN'S HANDS (TRADITIONAL VIEW)

TRADITIONAL MANNERS DICTATED THAT WOMEN BE TREATED AS THOUGH THEIR HANDS WERE JUST SCRUBBED FOR SURGERY.

WOMEN COULD NOT TOUCH DOORKNOBS

S. Adams

WOMEN COULD NOT TOUCH CHAIRS

WOMEN COULD NOT TOUCH MONEY

MOST DOLLAR BILLS HAVE BEEN IN PEOPLE'S NOSES.

WOMEN'S HANDS (MODERN VIEW)

THE MODERN VIEW IS THAT WOMEN SHOULD TOUCH ALL THE SAME OBJECTS AS MEN. THE ONLY PROBLEM IS WHEN MODERN MEN DATE TRADITIONAL WOMEN.

S. Adams

WOMEN **CAN** TOUCH DOORKNOBS

WATCH OUT FOR THE DOOR.

WHUMP!

UNH

WOMEN **CAN** TOUCH CHAIRS

HER CHAIR IS BETTER. I'LL TAKE IT FOR MY SIDE.

WOMEN **CAN** TOUCH MONEY

HERE'S MY HALF. MAYBE YOU CAN WASH DISHES WITH YOUR ELBOWS FOR YOUR SHARE.

LAUGHING AT TRAGEDY

IT IS NOT POLITE TO LAUGH AT THE MISFORTUNE OF OTHERS, UNLESS IT BECOMES A HEALTH RISK TO CONTAIN IT.

IT WAS TWO YEARS AGO THAT I LOST MY HUSBAND AT "JUNGLE SAFARI WORLD."

I SAID, "HONEY, PLEASE DON'T MOON THE CHEETAHS. THEY LOOK FAST."

DON'T LAUGH.

SOME PEOPLE THINK IT WAS "FUNNY."

LAUGHTER AS DEFLECTION

YOU MAY USE LAUGHTER AS A POLITE WAY TO DEFLECT UNWANTED INVITATIONS.

TRY A SMALL LAUGH FIRST.

I WAS THINKING MAYBE WE COULD GO TO A MOVIE.

HEH-HEH HEH

IF THE OFFENDER DOES NOT GET THE HINT, ESCALATE.

MAYBE SATURDAY?

HA HA HA HA HA

IF THIS TECHNIQUE DOES NOT PRODUCE RESULTS, QUIT BEFORE IT GETS UGLY.

I LIKE A WOMAN WHO CAN LAUGH EASILY.

HA-HA

BORES AT MEETINGS

THERE ARE THREE POLITE METHODS FOR DEALING WITH BORES AT MEETINGS.

FEEL FREE TO HAVE SIDE CONVERSATIONS IF YOU NEITHER FEAR NOR RESPECT THE PERSON SPEAKING.

BRING CRUNCHY FOOD AND TRY TO DROWN OUT THE SPEAKER.

INTERRUPT FREQUENTLY SO YOU CAN USE UP THE MEETING TIME WITH YOUR OWN LONG-WINDED STORIES.

BORING OTHER PEOPLE

IF YOU ARE BORING AND DON'T KNOW IT, USE THESE VISUAL CUES TO KNOW WHEN YOUR STORY HAS GONE ON TOO LONG.

STAGE ONE OF BOREDOM IS CHARACTERIZED BY SHRINKING PUPILS AND A ZOMBIE-LIKE STIFFNESS.

...SO I TRIED THE MATH COPROCESSOR SOCKET AND...

STAGE TWO OF BOREDOM IS CHARACTERIZED BY THE EYES ROLLING BACK IN THE HEAD AND A LOSS OF BALANCE.

...SO I SAID "WHO BURNED THESE EPROMS IN ANYWAY?"

IF YOU GET TO STAGE THREE, YOU MIGHT AS WELL JUST GO AHEAD AND FINISH YOUR STORY.

...AND THAT WASN'T EVEN THE INTERESTING PART!

DEALING WITH BORES

IN THE OLD DAYS, BEFORE TELEVISION, BORES WERE TOLERATED BECAUSE THERE WAS NOTHING BETTER TO DO. BUT IN THESE BUSY TIMES IT IS NECESSARY TO POLITELY DISMISS THEM.

SHOO!

... SO THEN I THOUGHT, WHY NOT EAT AN APPLE? SO, BELIEVE IT OR NOT, THAT'S JUST WHAT I DID. THEN I THOUGHT...

WAIT! STOP!

S. Adams

NO OFFENSE, BUT YOU'RE BORING ME TO DEATH. IF YOU CAN'T COME UP WITH SOMETHING INTEREST-ING THEN I'LL HAVE TO ASK YOU TO SHUT UP.

GEE, I'M SORRY.

NOPE. NOT INTERESTING. I HAVE TO ASK YOU TO SHUT UP NOW.

DISCOURAGING A SERIAL TALKER

A "SERIAL TALKER" IS A PERSON WHO CAN TALK CONSTANTLY AND FOREVER WITHOUT PAUSING FOR TOPIC SHIFTS. YOU MUST DISCOURAGE THEM.

SUBTLE HINTS DO NOT WORK.

NOTICE THE SERIAL TALKER'S TRANCE STATE

YAK YAK YAK

NEWS

HIDING WILL NOT WORK.

THEY WILL FOLLOW YOU ANYWHERE

YAK YAK YAK YAK YAK

THE ONLY KNOWN SOLUTION IS TO PLUG THE HOLE.

DANG! THIS ONE KNOWS SIGN LANGAUGE!

YAK YAK YAK

EXCUSING YOURSELF FROM BORES

YOU CAN AVOID PROLONGED INTERACTION. WITH BORES BY USING THESE ESCAPE TACTICS.

SIGNAL YOUR DISTRESS AND HOPE AN INTERESTING PERSON WILL COME TO YOUR RESCUE.

BLAH BLAH

YAWN

HE NEEDS HELP.

S. Adams

CARRY AN EMPTY GLASS WITH YOU AT ALL TIMES.

OOH... I'D BETTER GET A REFILL.

FIND AN UNWITTING REPLACEMENT AND EXCUSE YOURSELF BECAUSE YOU'VE "ALREADY HEARD THE STORY."

TELL THAT STORY AGAIN FOR JOSH.

PARENTS AND CHILDREN
ACKNOWLEDGING THE DIFFERENT CHILD

IF ONE CHILD IN THE FAMILY HAS NO RESEMBLANCE TO THE OTHERS, IT'S BEST TO LEAVE THE TOPIC ALONE.

THESE ARE MY SONS, JOHNNY, JACK AND BIFF.

IT CAN BE EMBARASSING TO SINGLE OUT A FAMILY MEMBER WHO LOOKS "DIFFERENT."

JOHNNY AND JACK LOOK JUST LIKE YOU... BUT BIFF... GEE, THAT'S UNUSUAL...

DON'T MAKE IT WORSE BY SPECULATING.

WAIT A MINUTE... IS YOUR GARBAGEMAN GUS SIMPSON?

BABYSITTING

IF FRIENDS IMPOSE ON YOU TO BABYSIT IT IS WITHIN YOUR RIGHTS TO CONVERT THE CHILD TO A NEW RELIGION.

THANKS FOR AGREEING TO BABYSIT, DOGBERT.

SHOO! HAVE FUN.

DAVE, YOUR PARENTS ARE HEATHENS. LET ME TEACH YOU THE WAYS OF DOGBERTISM.

S. Adams

LATER

THANKS, DOGBERT. WE WON'T IMPOSE ON YOU LIKE THAT AGAIN.

I WOULDN'T THINK SO.

DOGBERT'S CLUES FOR THE CLUELESS

BRAGGING ABOUT YOUR KID

WHEN PARENTS BRAG ABOUT THEIR KIDS, YOU HAVE AN OBLIGATION TO BRING THEM GENTLY BACK TO REALITY.

THIS IS MY YOUNGEST SON, TIMMY. HE'S A GENIUS.

WELL, I WOULDN'T BE <u>TOO</u> PROUD. LOOK AT THE EARS ON THIS KID! THEY'RE HUGE!

NOTE: AFTER YOU MAKE YOUR POINT, IT'S POLITE TO STOP.

DOES YOUR HUSBAND KNOW YOU WERE DATING "DUMBO" THE FLYING ELEPHANT?

RESPECT YOUR PARENTS

SHOW RESPECT FOR YOUR PARENTS BY AVOIDING THESE BEHAVIORS.

DON'T TRY TO TRICK THEM INTO THINKING YOU'RE NOT RELATED TO THEM.

I THINK YOU'RE OLD ENOUGH TO KNOW... I'M ADOPTED.

DON'T MAKE THEM GRAND-PARENTS IN THEIR THIRTIES

SAY HI TO GRAMPS AND GRANNY.

Fossils

DON'T MAKE THEM HAVE TO PRETEND THEY'RE OPEN-MINDED.

BRENT IS A COWBOY!

EMBARRASSING STORIES

YOUR MOTHER HAS A LIFETIME RIGHT TO TELL EMBARRASSING STORIES ABOUT YOU.

DID I EVER TELL YOU THE CUTE STORY ABOUT JEFFREY'S FIRST VISIT TO THE ZOO?

HA HA! WELL, JEFFREY WAS JUST REACHING PUBERTY, AND STILL CONFUSED ABOUT A LOT OF THINGS...

NO NO PLEASE!!!

LATER

... AND TO THIS DAY HE'S STILL BANNED FROM THE MONKEY CAGE AREA.

GRANDPARENTS AND GRANDCHILDREN

GRANDPARENTS MAY SEEK REVENGE ON THEIR CHILDREN BY HOW THEY TREAT THE GRANDCHILDREN.

GRANDPARENTS MAY ONE-UP THEIR CHILDREN'S GIFTS.

G.I. JOE

KEYS TO YOUR AMPHIBIOUS ASSAULT VEHICLE.

GRANDPARENTS MAY TELL STORIES TO REMOVE ANY SHRED OF RESPECT THE CHILDREN MIGHT HAVE FOR THEIR PARENTS.

YOUR DAD TRIED OUT FOR THE GIRL'S BASKETBALL TEAM, BUT HE DIDN'T MAKE IT.

GRANDPARENTS MAY SPOIL THE GRANDCHILDREN WITH LOW LEVELS OF DISCIPLINE.

I'M NAKED AND I'M GOING TO HITCH-HIKE TO NORWAY.

HAVE FUN, DEAR.

MOTHERS VERSUS FATHERS

IT IS NOT POLITE TO INSULT A PERSON'S MOTHER. HOWEVER, FATHERS ARE FAIR GAME.

YOUR FATHER IS SO DUMB HE DRIVES HIS CAR BACKWARD TO REFILL THE GAS TANK.

HE'S THE ONLY PERSON WHO EVER BOUGHT AN INDOOR KITE.

S. Adams

HE WAITED YEARS TO HAVE CHILDREN BECAUSE HE THOUGHT IT WAS WRONG TO SLEEP WITH A MARRIED WOMAN.

HEY! IS THAT AN INSULT TO MY MOTHER?

ASHES OF THE DEPARTED

Panel 1:
CREMATION WAS INVENTED AFTER ETIQUETTE, SO MOST ETIQUETTE BOOKS LACK THESE IMPORTANT TIPS.

S. Adams

Panel 2:
DON'T SNEEZE WHEN THE LID IS OFF.

GESUNDHEIT.

Panel 3:
DON'T EXPLAIN THE TECHNICAL ASPECTS EVEN IF YOU KNOW THEM.

IT'S LIKE YOUR BARBECUE, BUT THEY DON'T USE STEAK SAUCE. I MEAN, WHY WOULD THEY? ANYWAY...

Panel 4:
NO MATTER HOW MUCH YOU NEED A FLOWER VASE, DON'T EVEN CONSIDER IT.

OF COURSE, HE'S DEAD WHEREAS THE FLOWERS ARE ALIVE...

FUNERAL ETIQUETTE

NEVER USE THE OPPORTUNITY OF SOMEBODY'S DEATH TO PLAY A PRACTICAL JOKE, UNLESS IT'S A REALLY GOOD ONE LIKE ONE OF THESE.

R.I.P.

S.Adams

THE "BORED TO DEATH" GAG

THAT WAS A GOOD STORY, BARRY, BUT I THINK ALICE WAS A BIT BORED.

THE "BREATHING" GAG

HE'S BREATHING!

THE "SCRATCHING TO GET OUT" GAG.

SCRATCH SCRATCH

ASKING "WHY AREN'T YOU MARRIED?"

WHEN MARRIED PEOPLE BADGER SINGLE PEOPLE ABOUT GETTING MARRIED, THE SINGLE PERSON MAY RESPOND IN TWO WAYS.

SO, BOB, WHEN ARE YOU GOING TO FIND SOME NICE WOMAN AND TIE THE KNOT?

WAAAHH!

S. Adams

WIMP RESPONSE

I HOPE THAT SOON I MAY IMITATE YOUR LIFESTYLE AND FIND THE MATE WHO CAN MAKE ME WHOLE.

AGGRESSIVE RESPONSE

GOSH, MAYBE IF I GET BORED DATING THE WALLENDA TRIPLETS I'LL JOIN YOU IN THE BOWELS OF HELL.

COMPLIMENTING A SPOUSE (WIFE)

IF SOMEBODY COMPLIMENTS YOUR WIFE, YOU MAY TAKE THE CREDIT YOURSELF.

YOUR WIFE IS VERY PRETTY.

THANK YOU VERY MUCH. I SELECTED HER BECAUSE SHE MATCHES MY FURNITURE.

BUT DON'T GO OVERBOARD

OF COURSE, YOU'VE GOT TO HAVE ONE OF THESE TO GET A WOMAN LIKE THAT!

S. Adams

SIGNIFICANT OTHER

UNMARRIED PEOPLE WHO LIVE TOGETHER SHOULD AVOID THESE MISTAKES...

DO NOT CAVE-IN TO SOCIETY'S VIEWS WHEN INTRODUCING YOUR "OTHER."

HI, I'M BOB, AND THIS IS THE GODLESS TRAMP THAT LIVES WITH ME.

DO NOT CONCOCT A RIDICULOUS FIB THAT ONLY YOUR PARENTS WOULD BE NAIVE ENOUGH TO BELIEVE.

MOM, DAD, THIS IS MY FRIEND ARNOLD. HE RENTS A ROOM IN MY APARTMENT.

DO NOT CLING STUBBORNLY TO YOUR LIBERAL VIEWS.

LINDA ISN'T COVERED BY MY MEDICAL PLAN AT WORK, BUT SHE'S BEEN A REAL TROOPER SINCE THE FISHING INCIDENT.

S. Adams

ANSWERING THE PHONE

TO BE A TELEPHONE RECEPTIONIST, LEARN THE THREE MAJOR BEHAVIORS WHICH ARE CONSIDERED GOOD MANNERS.

SPEAK LIKE A ZOMBIE ON A COFFEE BUZZ AND HIT "HOLD."

HELLOUNITEDCONGLOMERATE IHATEMYJOBSOPLEASEHOLD.

CLICK

ACT LIKE TAKING A MESSAGE WOULD BE A MAJOR BOTHER.

SIGH⚙ THAT WOULD REQUIRE PAPER... AND A WRITING THING... I COULD CHECK AROUND...

ACT LIKE A TEMP WORKER WHO WAS TRANSPORTED INTO THE BUILDING IN A SEALED BAG.

I DON'T KNOW WHO DOES THAT... I DON'T KNOW OUR ADDRESS... I DON'T KNOW WHAT PRODUCTS WE MAKE.

TAKING CALLS

YOU CAN MAKE PEOPLE FEEL INSIGNIFICANT BY ANSWERING YOUR PHONE WHILE THEY'RE IN YOUR OFFICE.

S. Adams

...AND SO, IT'S CLEAR THAT WE HAVE THREE OPTIONS...

RRRING

EXCUSE ME, THIS IS PROBABLY SOMETHING MORE IMPORTANT THAN YOU. FEEL FREE TO STARE OUT MY WINDOW.

UH...

RRRING

NO, NO PROBLEM. THIS IS A GOOD TIME TO TALK...

VOICE MAIL ETIQUETTE

VOICE MAIL IS A GOOD WAY TO POLITELY BLOW OFF PEOPLE YOU'D RATHER NOT SPEAK TO.

LEAVE A MESSAGE THAT INSTILLS HOPELESSNESS AND DESPAIR IN THE CALLER.

...I'M NOT HERE. IF THIS IS AN EMERGENCY CALL JACKIE...HA HA... AS IF SHE ANSWERS HER PHONE.

BEEP

LEAVE CONFUSING AUDIO MENU CHOICES.

...BUT IF YOU HAVE TYPE "AB" NEGATIVE BLOOD AND YOU'RE TALL BUT NOT BLONDE PRESS THE SQUARE ROOT OF 42 ON YOUR KEYPAD...

RETURN YOUR VOICE MAIL CALLS DURING LUNCH TO AVOID GETTING A LIVE PERSON. THEN LEAVE ILLOGICAL ANSWERS TO THEIR QUESTIONS.

THE ANSWER TO YOUR QUESTION IS "TROUT." I HOPE THAT HELPS.

WHEN TO CALL

PEOPLE DON'T SIT AROUND WAITING FOR YOUR CALL; THEY'RE ALWAYS BUSY. YOU MUST LEARN WHICH ACTIVITIES ARE BEST TO INTERRUPT.

DON'T CALL DURING DINNER— PEOPLE ARE HARD TO UNDERSTAND.

BONT CHLOL BLURING MINNER, MLUTHEAD!!

DON'T CALL FROM 9 PM TO 11 PM UNLESS YOU WANT EVERYBODY'S PERSONAL LIFE TO BE JUST LIKE YOURS.

SO, WHAT ARE YOU DOING?

THE BEST TIME TO CALL IS AT 3 AM. THAT WAY THE CALLEE THINKS IT'S AN EMERGENCY AND GIVES YOU FULL ATTENTION.

SO, WHAT ARE YOU DOING?

GIVING CASH

CASH IS A PERFECTLY ACCEPTABLE GIFT AS LONG AS YOU AVOID THESE MISTAKES.

STICK TO ROUND NUMBERS.

HAPPY BIRTHDAY HONEY. I GOT YOU SEVENTEEN DOLLARS AND... LET'S SEE...

DON'T TRY TO MIX CUSTOMS.

WHY IS IT ALL COVERED BY INK?

I DIDN'T WANT YOU TO KNOW HOW MUCH I SPENT.

DON'T ASK FOR A RECEIPT.

I'D LIKE YOU TO COUNT IT AND THEN INITIAL THIS FORM.

HOME-MADE GIFTS

YOU CAN MAKE POLITE PEOPLE UNHAPPY BY GIVING THEM HOME-MADE GIFTS TO DECORATE THEIR HOMES.

IMPOSE YOUR HOBBIES ON OTHER PEOPLE'S HOMES.

I TRIED TO CAPTURE THE MOST COLORFUL MOMENT IN DUCK HUNTING... AND IT'S ALL YOURS.

PERSONALIZE THE GIFT TO MAKE IT HARD TO GIVE AWAY.

IT'S YOUR HOUSE, MADE ENTIRELY FROM PASTA!

SOLVE YOUR RECYCLING PROBLEM AND ANNOY YOUR FRIENDS AT THE SAME TIME.

ALL YOU NEED IS A LAMP SHADE!

BOTTLES

SELECTIVE INVITATIONS

USE THESE TRICKS TO
AVOID INVITING AN
UNPOPULAR CO-WORKER
TO YOUR PARTY.

THE FLAWED DIRECTIONS TRICK

IS THIS MAP RIGHT?
DO YOU REALLY LIVE
IN NEW ZEALAND?

S. Adams

EMPHASIZE THE POSITIVE

CONGRATULATIONS!
YOU MADE THE LIST
OF ALTERNATES. IF
SOMEBODY DIES DURING
THE PARTY WE'LL CALL
YOU!

YES!

SPECIALLY TRAINED DOGS CAN
CUT THE UNDESIRABLES FROM
THE HERD.

I HOPE YOU
ALL CAN MAKE
IT.

GIFTS FOR PARTIES

FOR SOME STRANGE REASON IT IS EXPECTED THAT GUESTS BRING GIFTS TO PARTIES.

GENERALLY, A HOST WILL KNOW IF YOUR GIFT IS SOMETHING YOU FOUND IN YOUR GLOVE COMPARTMENT.

A BREATH MINT STUCK TO A MAP. GEE.

AVOID GIFTS WHICH REQUIRE ANY SPECIAL MAINTENANCE.

LOOK, HONEY, IT'S A BALD EAGLE.

HOLD ONTO YOUR GIFT UNTIL YOU'RE SURE THE PARTY IS WORTH IT.

NOT SO FAST. I'D LIKE TO LOOK AROUND FIRST.

S. Adams

ENTERTAINING GUESTS

GUESTS ARE ANNOYING. THEY EAT YOUR FOOD AND MAKE YOU MISS GOOD TELEVISION SHOWS. USE THESE TRICKS TO AVOID REPEAT VISITS.

WE USED TO JUST THROW AWAY THE SOAP BARS WHEN THEY GOT SMALL.

HAVE YOU HEARD THE DIGITALLY REMASTERED "TINY TIM" CLASSICS?

WHICH WAY TO YOUR BATHROOM?

I DON'T HAVE ONE.

BAD GIFTS

DO NOT SIT PASSIVELY AND ACT LIKE YOU ENJOY A POORLY THOUGHT OUT GIFT.

BE HONEST

SHODDY CRAFTSMANSHIP, HAPHAZARD DESIGN... YEAH, I THINK IT'S TIME TO CONSIDER ADOPTION.

SOME GIFTS — LIKE TUBE SOCKS AND A PAPER WEIGHT — CAN BE COMBINED TO MAKE ONE GOOD GIFT.

SOMETIMES YOU CAN FIND A WAY TO GET ENJOYMENT FROM PURELY PRACTICAL GIFTS.

THANKS FOR THE GRAVY BOAT, SWEETHEART.

LOSING GRACEFULLY

THERE'S NO SUCH THING AS "LOSING GRACEFULLY." TRY THESE METHODS INSTEAD.

MINIMIZE THE IMPORTANCE OF THE LOSS.

CHESS IS FOR DORKS.

HIDE THE RULEBOOK BEFORE THE GAME AND CLAIM VICTORY ON A TECHNICALITY.

THERE... I WIN.

BUT WAIT! YOU'VE ILLEGALLY PASSED PAWN WITH ROOK WHILE QUEEN HAS PMS.

CHEAT AND ACT INDIGNANT IF CAUGHT.

I HAD A QUEEN BEFORE I WENT TO THE BATHROOM!

WHAT ARE YOU SUGGESTING??!

PEER PRESSURE

PEER PRESSURE IS WHAT YOU DO TO PEOPLE WHO ARE NOT, IN YOUR OPINION, PEERS.

S. Adams

YOU CAN CREATE YOUR OWN FUN WITH PEER PRESSURE.

I'LL BET YOU'RE NOT SOBER ENOUGH TO DISASSEMBLE YOUR CAR IN THE DRIVEWAY.

IT MAY BE NECESSARY TO GLAMORIZE AN ACTIVITY TO GET OTHERS TO JOIN IN.

IT MAKES YOU COUGH AND STINK AND DIE. TRY IT!

WHAT HAVE I GOT TO LOSE?

THERE IS NO LOGICAL LIMIT TO THE FUN YOU CAN HAVE WITH PEER PRESSURE.

DON'T BE A WUSS. YOU CAN PULL OUT BEFORE IT HARDENS IF YOU GET SCARED.

WET CEMENT

PET ETIQUETTE

HEY! THIS ISN'T FUNNY.

S. Adams

TIP #1: TRY TO MINIMIZE THE INAPPROPRIATE ACTIONS OF YOUR PET.

THAT JUST MEANS HE LIKES YOU.

TIP #2: TAKE YOUR PET'S SIDE.

I USED TO DISCOURAGE THAT BEHAVIOR, BUT IF YOU THINK ABOUT IT THEY REALLY DON'T ASK FOR MUCH OUT OF LIFE...

TIP #3: LIE TO PROTECT YOUR PET FROM BLAME.

THAT WAS THERE BEFORE WE CAME OVER.

SHAKING HANDS

TRY TO AVOID THESE EMBARRASSING SITUATIONS WHEN SHAKING HANDS.

IT IS IMPOLITE TO TOWEL OFF AFTER SHAKING HANDS, NO MATTER HOW CLAMMY IT WAS.

THAT WAS PRETTY GROSS.

IN A BUSINESS SETTING IT IS NEVER APPROPRIATE TO MAKE WEAK PEOPLE BEG FOR MERCY.

BARK LIKE A DOG.

CRUNCH

IT IS IMPOLITE FOR A MAN TO EXTEND HIS HAND UNLESS THE WOMAN MAKES THE FIRST MOVE.

DANG! FAKED OUT AGAIN.

S. Adams

THANK YOU NOTES

SOME PEOPLE FOLLOW AN ANCIENT PRACTICE OF WRITING THANK YOU NOTES. THEY MUST BE STOPPED.

WELL-BRED PEOPLE WITH TINY NOSES WRITE PERSONAL NOTES TO THANK PEOPLE FOR ANYTHING.

thank you for selling those tires to me. I shall cherish them always.

THE WELL-BRED PEOPLE WITH TINY NOSES MUST BE LOCATED AND STOPPED.

SHE'S HERE.

EVENTUALLY WE CAN RID THE WORLD OF THIS OUT-DATED AND INEFFICIENT PRACTICE, THUS REDUCING THE EXPECTATIONS ON THE REST OF US.

VACATION PICTURES

REMEMBER THESE TIPS WHEN LOOKING AT PEOPLE'S BORING VACATION PICTURES.

DON'T GUESS WHAT THE PICTURE IS SUPPOSED TO BE.

HEY, IT'S A WALRUS... WEARING YOUR BEACH HAT... OH...

SARCASM IS OKAY BECAUSE IT WILL GO COMPLETELY UNNOTICED.

DO YOU HAVE ANY MORE PICTURES OF FLORIDA CLOUDS? THEY'RE SO DIFFERENT!

ISN'T IT AMAZING?

DON'T QUESTION A PERSON'S PHOTOGRAPHIC TALENT.

I DON'T THINK A PHOTO OF THE MONA LISA IS ART IN ITSELF.

DIDN'T YOU NOTICE I USED BLACK AND WHITE FILM?

S. Adams

RECOGNIZING FINE ART

YOU WOULDN'T KNOW FINE ART IF IT BACKED OVER YOUR HEAD WITH A TRUCK. USE THESE CLUES TO KNOW WHEN YOU SEE IT.

IT'S "FINE ART" IF THE MALE PERFORMERS WEAR TIGHTS.

I ADORE SHAKESPEARE, AND I LOVE THE BALLET.

THERE'S A PATTERN HERE.

IT'S "FINE ART" WHEN PEOPLE WITH EATING DISORDERS DON COSTUMES AND SHOUT AT EACH OTHER IN ITALIAN.

AND OPERA ALWAYS MAKES ME WEEP.

WELL, IT BORES ME TOO, BUT YOU DON'T SEE ME CRYING ABOUT IT.

PAINTINGS OF "FINE ART" ARE THOSE DONE BY ARTISTS WHO ARE EITHER INSANE OR AT LEAST VERY SENSITIVE.

THE ARTIST HANGED HIMSELF BECAUSE OF A BAD HAIRCUT.

FINE ART.

CLEANING FOR COMPANY

SOMETIMES YOU GET SO ACCUSTOMED TO YOUR OWN FILTH THAT YOU DON'T SEE IT. USE THESE CLUES TO TELL WHEN YOU SHOULD TIDY UP FOR GUESTS.

CLUE #1: THE SHOWER HEAD IS SHORTER THAN IT USED TO BE AND THERE ARE STALACTITES.

CLUE #2: IT BECOMES INCREASINGLY DIFFICULT TO TELL THE BABY FROM THE CAT.

CLUE #3: THE PARAKEET DIES AND YOU ACCIDENTALLY BURY IT IN THE DINING ROOM.

BORROWING STUFF

IF YOU FIND SOMEBODY NICE ENOUGH TO LEND HIS POSSESSIONS, GET ALL YOU CAN BEFORE SOMEBODY ELSE DOES.

I NOTICED YOU WEREN'T USING YOUR FAMILY SO I DECIDED TO BORROW THEM.

HEY, IT FEELS LIKE YOU'RE NOT EVEN USING A LOT OF THESE INTERNAL ORGANS.

I CAN'T BELIEVE THERE WAS SO MUCH GOOD STUFF LEFT.

FLAUNTING YOUR WEALTH

NO MATTER WHAT YOUR INCOME, THERE IS SOMEBODY POORER TO MAKE YOU FEEL SUPERIOR.

USE THESE TECHNIQUES TO RUB IT IN.

COMPLAIN ABOUT YOUR TAX BURDEN.

IF NOT FOR MY SIX HOMES, THE TAXES WOULD EAT ME ALIVE.

I WISH.

S. Adams

BRAG ABOUT YOUR FOOLISH CONSUMER HABITS.

I ONLY USE "SUPREME ULTRA UNLEADED" GAS. IT'S THE SAME AS "UNLEADED" BUT WITH A MUCH COOLER NAME.

COMPARE YOU ASSETS, FEATURE BY FEATURE.

DOES THAT MODEL HAVE "PICTURE IN PICTURE"?

COLOR TV

SUFFERING FOOLS

USE THESE METHODS TO POLITELY ENDURE THE FOOLS IN YOUR LIFE.

TO KEEP FROM KILLING THEM, TRY READING AND HUMMING AS A DISTRACTION.

WHAT IF ALL THE PEOPLE ON WELFARE BECAME LAWYERS? PROBLEM SOLVED.

HMM HMM HMM

S. Adams

IT IS NOT YET POLITE TO USE ELECTRIC STUN GUNS ON FOOLS. HOWEVER, IF ENOUGH PEOPLE DO IT, IT BECOMES ACCEPTABLE BASED ON THE PRINCIPAL OF "COMMON USAGE."

YOUR BEST BET IS TO FIND A WAY TO TRAP ALL THE FOOLS IN ONE PLACE, THEN LEAVE.

BARGAINS

FLEA MARKET

OTHER RELIGIONS

NEVER DISCUSS RELIGION WITH THOSE WHO ARE SO IGNORANT THEY DON'T SUBSCRIBE TO YOUR BELIEFS.

NEVER MIX LOGIC AND RELIGION.

...BUT IF HE'S OMNIPOTENT AND HE CREATED ME, IT MUST BE HIS FAULT IF I SIN.

LET ME PUT IT THIS WAY: SHUT UP.

S. Adams

DON'T MAKE JOKES ABOUT GOD TO PEOPLE WHO ARE NERVOUS ABOUT RETRIBUTION.

I USED TO HEAR GOD'S VOICE ALL THE TIME. BUT I TALKED HIM INTO PLAYING "EASY LISTENING" MUSIC INSTEAD.

AND DID I MENTION NEVER TO MIX LOGIC AND RELIGION?

WHAT HAPPENS TO THE FOUR BILLION PEOPLE WHO DON'T KNOW THAT GOD LOVES ALL HIS CHILDREN?

ETERNAL HELL.

SMOKERS

SMOKERS HAVE NO SENSE OF SOCIAL CONSCIENCE. THEY CAN RATIONALIZE ANYTHING AS BEING ACCEPTABLE BEHAVIOR.

S. Adams

IN OUTDOOR TICKET LINES

MY SMOKE IS DISSIPATING HARMLESSLY IN THE AIR. NOBODY EVEN NOTICES.

IN RESTAURANTS

WE GOT OUR SECTION, THEY GOT THEIRS. EVERYBODY'S HAPPY.

NO SMOKING SECTION

ASKING PERMISSION

DO YOU MIND IF I RUIN YOUR LUNGS AND MAKE YOU STINK, OR DO YOU WANT A CAREER HERE?

OTHER PEOPLE'S ETHNICITY

NEVER MAKE ASSUMP-
TIONS ABOUT THE
ETHNIC ORIGINS OF
OTHER PEOPLE.

S. Adams

...THIS PART OF THE
APPLICATION ASKS
FOR YOUR ETHNIC
GROUP.

WRONG

I'LL JUST PUT "POOR
WHITE TRASH" UNLESS
THERE'S SOMETHING
MORE SPECIFIC.

MAKING IT WORSE

ALWAYS REMEMBER,
YOU HAVE AS MUCH
RIGHT TO BE PROUD
OF YOUR HERITAGE
AS ANYBODY ELSE.

WHEN PEOPLE TRY TO MERGE IN FRONT OF YOU, THEY ARE, IN EFFECT, CALLING YOU A "WUSS." YOU HAVE THE RIGHT TO KILL THEM.

HE'S TRYING TO MERGE. HE MUST BE STOPPED.

AAAH!

HOWEVER IT IS STILL CONSIDERED IMPOLITE TO FLASH THE "I'M NUMBER ONE" SIGN AFTERWARD.

PUBLIC LAUNDRY ETIQUETTE

PUBLIC LAUNDRY FACILITIES HAVE SPECIAL RULES OF ETIQUETTE.

THERE IS NO DRESS CODE. YOU CAN WEAR ANYTHING THAT IS STILL CLEAN.

IF SOMEBODY LEAVES THEIR LAUNDRY IN THE WASHER THAT YOU WANT, YOU HAVE THE RIGHT TO SCULPT A LAUNDRY BUNNY WITH THEIR STUFF.

NO MATTER HOW BORED YOU GET, IT IS NOT ACCEPTABLE TO TALK THE NIGHT JANITOR INTO TAKING A DRYER RIDE.

IT'S ONLY TWENTY-FIVE CENTS!

WEDGIES

MANY PEOPLE ASK ME, "DOGBERT, WHEN IS IT OKAY TO GIVE A WEDGIE?"

S. Adams

AFTER GETTING A TICKET

AFTER RECEIVING YOUR ANNUAL JOB PERFORMANCE EVALUATION.

THANKS FOR THE FEEDBACK!

AFTER AN ESPECIALLY BORING DATE

SWEARING

POLITE SOCIETY IS ACCEPTING MORE AND MORE SWEARING. YOU MUST TRY HARDER IF YOU WISH TO SHOCK.

IN THE OLD DAYS, SWEARING WOULD EASILY SHOCK PEOPLE.

BULL FEATHERS

THESE DAYS THE TRADITIONAL SHOCKING WORDS ARE OVER-USED AND INEFFECTIVE.

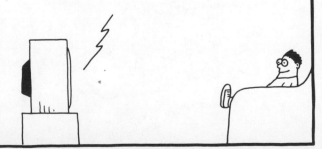

AND IN THE WEATHER, IT LOOKS LIKE A *!@☆% DAY TOMORROW.

SO IN ORDER TO SHOCK SOME-ONE YOU MUST CHOOSE WORDS SO VILE THEY CAUSE PEOPLE AND THEIR PETS TO CATCH FIRE.

I THINK I MADE MY POINT.

AAAGH

EXCUSE ME

OVER TIME, THE PHRASE "EXCUSE ME" HAS CHANGED FROM BEING A WIMPY REQUEST TO BEING A SARCASTIC REMARK.

IN THE EARLY DAYS (ENGLAND)

EXCUSETH ME, PLEASE, KIND SIR.

IT DOTH BE MY PLEASURE.

EVENTUALLY IT BECAME A COMMAND MEANING "GET OUT OF MY WAY."

'SCUSE ME.

NOW IT IS ACCEPTED AS A SARCASTIC REMARK.

EXCU-U-U-SE ME!

DOGBERT'S CLUES FOR THE CLUELESS

KNOWING WHAT TO SAY

QUIET SUFFERING

WHEN SOMEBODY SAYS "HOW ARE YOU," IT IS IMPOLITE TO ANSWER HONESTLY.

HI, LARRY, HOW ARE YOU?

WRONG

I'VE GOT A WICKED CASE OF JOCK ITCH. MY WIFE IS DATING MY BROTHER. I THINK I'M ATTRACTED TO MEN.

CORRECT

OH, CAN'T COMPLAIN. HOW 'BOUT YOU?

THE OPEN ZIPPER

IT IS YOUR DUTY TO DISCREETLY INFORM A MAN IF HIS TROUSER ZIPPER IS DOWN. USE CUTE TERMS TO MINIMIZE THE EMBARRASSMENT.

EXCUSE ME, BUT YOU'RE "FLYING LOW."

WHAT?

LET'S SEE, UH...

MISTER ED IS LEAVING THE BARN?

THE SHUTTLE BAY DOOR IS OPEN?

WILLY'S GOING TO THE CIRCUS?

WHAT ARE YOU TALK-ING ABOUT?

IF THAT DOESN'T WORK, TRY GUIDED IMAGERY.

YOU ARE IN A HOTEL IN PARIS ... THE CURTAINS SHOULD BE CLOSED BUT INSTEAD YOU SEE THE EIFFEL TOWER OUTSIDE...

BAD HAIRPIECES

WHEN CONFRONTED WITH A BAD HAIRPIECE TRY TO AVOID THESE MISTAKES.

NO MATTER HOW TEMPTING, DO NOT SLAP IT OFF.

DON'T BE CONDESCENDING, UNLESS YOU DISGUISE IT AS SARCASM.

IT MUST BE TOUGH TO HAVE SO MUCH TESTOSTERONE COURSING THROUGH YOUR VEINS.

DO NOT BECOME OBSESSED BY THE HAIRPIECE AND STARE TRANSFIXED WHILE TALKING.

WHAT THE HECK IS HE THINKING?

I THINK SHE'S AROUSED.

IF YOU CAN'T SAY SOME-
THING NICE ABOUT A
PERSON THEN AT LEAST
SAY IT BEHIND HIS
BACK.

I ONCE HAD A DATE
THAT WAS SO BORING
I ALMOST JUMPED
OUT A WINDOW TO
GET AWAY.

BUT THEN I THOUGHT
HA! HE'S SO CLUELESS
I CAN HAVE FUN BY
MOCKING HIM IN FRONT
OF OTHER PEOPLE.

LUCKY FOR YOU
THAT YOU'RE
DATING ME
NOW.

FAKING SYMPATHY

BEING POLITE MEANS OFTEN HAVING TO PRETEND THAT YOU CARE ABOUT OTHER PEOPLE'S PROBLEMS.

S. Adams

SINCERE SOUNDING SYMPATHY ALWAYS USES MORE THAN ONE WORD.

...WE LOST THE FARM AND WE ALL HAVE METAL PLATES IN OUR HEADS.

BUMMER.

OTHER PEOPLE'S PROBLEMS ARE BORING. TRY DISGUISING YOUR YAWNS AS CRIES OF SYMPATHY.

HE CARES.

YAAARGH!!

TRY TO TOP THEIR STORY WITH TALES OF YOUR OWN WOE.

SO THEN I ...

I THINK I'M GETTING NEAR-SIGHTED IN ONE EYE.

FOREIGN LANGUAGES

IT IS RUDE TO SPEAK A FOREIGN LANGUAGE IN FRONT OF SOMEBODY, BUT IT IS NOT WITHOUT ADVANTAGES.

RUDE

XMPHLACA BI FLUCALAKA UN BIJNANA Y AQUAHOLDER*

GNE!

BUS STOP

*HIS HEAD IS LIKE A BUCKET

VERY RUDE

UCKET-BAY EAD-HAY.

ES-YAY

BUS STOP

EXTREMELY RUDE

SEE, WALTER? IF YOU TURN THIS BUCKET UPSIDE DOWN AND PUT YOUR GLASSES ON IT ... IT'S HIM!

BUS STOP

DISABILITIES

IT IS ACCEPTABLE TO INQUIRE ABOUT A PERSON'S DISABILITY ONLY IF THE DISABILITY IS ON THE "APPROVED" LIST.

VISION-IMPAIRED IS OKAY.

HOW LONG HAVE YOU BEEN VISION-IMPAIRED?

I'M NOT. I'M JUST FOND OF THE LOOK.

AWARENESS-IMPAIRED IS <u>NOT</u> ON THE APPROVED LIST.

HOW LONG HAVE YOU BEEN THIS WAY?

WHAT WAY?

ATTRACTIVENESS-IMPAIRED IS <u>NOT</u> ON THE LIST EITHER.

HOW LONG HAVE YOU HAD THIS PROBLEM?

FORGETTING NAMES

IF YOU FORGET SOMEBODY'S NAME IT IS ALWAYS BETTER NOT TO GUESS.

HI DILBERT!

HI ... UH... HOW'S IT GOING?

DOESN'T HE REMEMBER MY NAME? WHY DIDN'T HE SAY "HI DAVE"?

THINK

AND IF YOU DO GUESS, AT LEAST GUESS SOMETHING THAT SOUNDS DIGNIFIED.

GOOBER?

CONSTRUCTIVE CRITICISM

CRITICISM IS OFTEN CONSTRUCTIVE BECAUSE IT MAKES YOU FEEL SUPERIOR WHEN YOU GIVE IT.

I WAS JUST NOTICING HOW UGLY YOU ARE COMPARED TO ME.

DIDN'T I SEE YOU IN THE MOVIE "MASK"?

HEY! I'M WITTIER THAN YOU TOO! MAN, I'M FEELING GOOD. THANKS!

S.Adams

NEVER SAY "IT _ _ _ _ _ "